Greatest Ever

Vegetarian

The All Time Top 20 Greatest Recipes

p

This is a Parragon Book
This edition published in 2002

Parragon
Queen Street House
4 Queen Street
Bath BA1 1HE, UK

ISBN: 0-75259-294-7

Printed in China

NOTE

This book uses metric and imperial measurements. Follow the same
units of measurement throughout; do not mix metric and imperial.
All spoon measurements are level: teaspoons are assumed to be 5 ml,
and tablespoons are assumed to be 15 ml. Unless otherwise stated,
milk is assumed to be full fat, eggs and individual vegetables such as
potatoes are medium, and pepper is freshly ground black pepper.

The times given for each recipe are an approximate guide only
because the preparation times may differ according to the techniques
used by different people and the cooking times may vary as a result
of the type of oven used. The preparation times include marinating,
chilling and freezing times, where appropriate.

Recipes using raw or very lightly cooked eggs should be
avoided by infants, the elderly, pregnant women, convalescents,
and anyone suffering from an illness.

CONTENTS

INTRODUCTION

A balanced diet is crucial to good health. When planning meals, it is important to achieve a good balance of nutrients – protein, carbohydrate, vitamins, minerals and some fat. This is especially true for vegetarians, who need to make sure they are eating enough protein by combining starchy foods such as potatoes and pasta with beans, lentils or nuts. Dairy products, pulses, seeds and vegetables provide the calcium, iron and vitamins needed in a meat-free diet.

These 20 recipes were chosen to appeal to vegetarians, almost-vegetarians and non-vegetarians alike. The aim is to show just how varied, colourful and flavoursome a vegetarian diet can be. It will be useful for would-be vegetarians uncertain about what to eat, students on a limited budget and anybody who is stumped over what food to serve to a vegetarian guest.

The recipes come from far and wide, including India, Mexico and Europe. There are also variations on more traditional fare, such as a Vegetable Toad-in-the-Hole – a quick, tasty, filling family meal in which it is guaranteed you won't miss the meat at all. They will become core dishes in your vegetarian repertoire – delicious and enjoyable meals which provide the perfect way to introduce your friends and family to meat-free eating.

carrots

Above: A diet rich in vegetables is also high in fibre, which helps to keep the digestive tract healthy and free of disease.

MAKING CHANGES

spinach

When cooking these recipes, feel free to substitute some ingredients to suit your specific preferences or dietary convictions. If you don't eat dairy products, for example, use soya milk in place of cow's milk, cream substitute instead of dairy cream and vegetable margarine rather than butter.

Most vegetarian foods are clearly labelled with a 'suitable for vegetarians' symbol. Look out for it, and check the ingredients list on the packaging if you are in any doubt.

aubergines

To enjoy the best – the most nourishing, tastiest and freshest vegetables – it is a good idea to get into the habit of using vegetables when they are in season. In many of the recipes in this book, you can easily substitute the main vegetables with alternatives. By following the basic method for making Wild Mushroom Risotto, for example, and using fresh asparagus spears instead of mushrooms, you can turn it into an equally flavoursome asparagus risotto.

broccoli

spring onions

pumpkin

potatoes

Organic produce

Although not as regular in shape or size or as clean as conventionally farmed vegetables, organic produce, grown without the use of artificial fertilizers or pesticides, generally have a superior flavour. It's even better if the vegetables are freshly picked.

mushrooms

eggs

THE VEGETARIAN CUPBOARD

lasagne

BASIC DRY GOODS

Vegetarian cooks always keep a good supply of eggs, cheeses and fresh fruit and vegetables in the fridge. But to put many delicious vegetarian dishes together they often need a base of rice, pasta or beans, so it is useful to have plenty of these basic ingredients at hand. Use the following information as a checklist when you need to replenish your stores.

spaghetti

Below: Mixing plant proteins by combining starchy foods with nuts and pulses will maintain a good level of protein in the diet.

Grains

A good variety of grains is essential. For rice, choose from long-grain, basmati, Italian arborio for making risotto and paella, and wild rice to add interest. Look out for fragrant Thai rice, jasmine rice and combinations of different varieties to add colour and texture to your dishes. Remember that brown rice is a better source of vitamin B1 and fibre, but takes longer to cook.

Other grains add variety to your diet. Try to include some pearl barley, millet, bulgur wheat, polenta (made from corn), oatmeal and cous-cous.

tricolour ruoti

wholemeal pasta

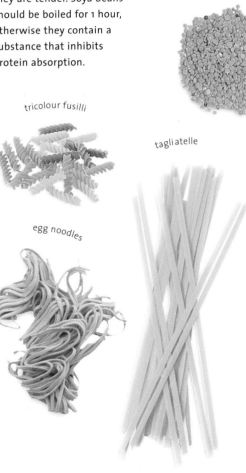

Pasta

Pasta is extremely popular so keep a good selection in stock. Always make sure you have the basic lasagne sheets, tagliatelle or fettucine (flat ribbons) and spaghetti. Try spinach- or tomato-flavoured varieties for a change, and sample some of the fresh pastas now available. Better still, make your own!

Legumes

Also called pulses, legumes are a valuable source of protein, vitamins and minerals. Stock up on soya beans, red kidney beans, cannellini beans, lentils, split peas and butter beans. Buying dried legumes which need soaking and cooking is cheaper, but canned ones are quicker and more convenient.

Cook dried red or black kidney beans in rapidly boiling water for 15 minutes to destroy harmful toxins in the outer skin. Drain and rinse the beans, and then simmer in fresh water until they are tender. Soya beans should be boiled for 1 hour, otherwise they contain a substance that inhibits protein absorption.

red lentils

tricolour fusilli

tagliatelle

egg noodles

tagliatelle verde

bay leaves

green chillies

tarragon

garlic

Vegetarian cooking relies on a good blend of herbs and spices to boost the flavour of the food. The addition of a few chopped nuts and seeds also makes a great deal of difference to the texture and protein content of many dishes. It is well worth keeping a wide range of these to add interest at a sprinkling.

VEGETARIAN FLAVOURINGS

sage

cinnamon

chilli seeds

Spices and herbs

As well as the basic spices, there are some exciting mixtures available – try Cajun, Chinese five-spice or one of the many curry blends. For the strongest flavour, grind your own spices in a mortar and pestle or a coffee mill. Don't leave ground spices in the cupboard for too long, as they may lose some of their flavour. It is better to buy small amounts as you need them.

Fresh herbs have a brighter, fresher flavour than dried herbs, but keep a few dried ones – such as thyme, rosemary and bay leaves – in your store-cupboard as a back-up. You can also grow basil, parsley, coriander and chives on a sunny windowsill, as long as you remember to water them regularly.

Chillies

These come both fresh and dried and in colours from green through yellow, orange and red to brown. Their hotness varies, so use with caution. As a guide, the smaller they are, the hotter they will be. The seeds are hottest and are usually discarded. Take care when cutting chillies not to rub your eyes with your fingers as the juice stings badly. Chilli powder should also be used sparingly.

Nuts and seeds

As well as adding protein, vitamins and valuable fats to the diet, nuts and seeds add flavour and texture. To really bring out the flavour of nuts and seeds, try toasting or dry-frying them until they are lightly browned.

red onions

basil

red chillies

coriander

Make sure that you keep a good supply of almonds, brazils, cashews, chestnuts (dried or canned), hazelnuts, peanuts, pecans, pistachios, pine kernels and walnuts. Coconut, either creamed or dessicated, is useful too. For your seed collection include sesame, sunflower, pumpkin and poppy as basic vegetarian ingredients.

Dried fruits

Currants, raisins, sultanas, dates, apples, apricots, figs, pears, prunes, peaches, mangoes, bananas and pineapples are all used in both savoury and sweet recipes. In preference, ok for untreated varieties – such as the darker unsulphured apricots, for example.

Oils and fats

Oils and fats are not just useful for cooking, but add a subtle flavour to the food and also contain some important vitamins – A, D, E and K – as well. Use a light olive oil for cooking, but have an extra-virgin olive oil in reserve to use in salad dressings. Sunflower oil is a good all-rounder for frying; sesame oil is wonderful in stir-fries; small doses of hazelnut and walnut oils are superb in salad dressings.

Mustards

Mustards are made from ground black, brown or white mustard seeds, blended with spices, then usually mixed to a paste with vinegar. Dijon mustard is medium hot and has a sharp flavour. Its versatility in salad dressings and marinades makes it ideal for vegetarians.

Vinegars

Choose three or four types of vinegar for your store-cupboard – red or white wine, cider, tarragon, sherry and balsamic offer a good range of flavours, and will add character to your dishes.

Bottled sauces

Soy sauce is widely used in Chinese and Southeast Asian cookery. Light soy sauce tends to be rather salty, whereas dark soy sauce is sweeter, and is more often used in dips and sauces. Black bean and yellow bean sauces add an instant authentic Chinese flavour to stir-fries.

root ginger

black bean sauce

olive oil

VEGETABLE TOAD-IN-THE-HOLE

>Serves 4   >Preparation time: 15 minutes   >Cooking time: 50–55 minutes

INGREDIENTS

BATTER

100 g/3½ oz plain flour

2 eggs, beaten

200 ml/7 fl oz milk

2 tbsp wholegrain mustard

2 tbsp vegetable oil

FILLING

2 tbsp butter

2 garlic cloves, crushed

1 onion, cut into eight pieces

75 g/2¾ oz baby carrots, halved lengthways

50 g/1¾ oz French beans

50 g/1¾ oz drained canned sweetcorn

2 tomatoes, seeded and cut into chunks

1 tsp wholegrain mustard

1 tbsp chopped fresh mixed herbs

salt and pepper

METHOD

1 To make the batter, sieve the flour and a pinch of salt into a large mixing bowl. Make a well in the centre and beat in the eggs and milk to make a batter. Stir in the mustard and leave to stand.

2 Pour the oil into a shallow ovenproof dish and heat in a preheated oven, 200°C/400°F/ Gas Mark 6, for 10 minutes.

3 To make the filling, melt the butter in a frying pan and sauté the garlic and onion for 2 minutes, stirring. Cook the carrots and beans in a saucepan of boiling water for 7 minutes or until tender. Drain well.

4 Add the sweetcorn and tomato to the frying pan with the mustard and herbs. Season well and add the carrots and beans.

5 Remove the dish from the oven. Pour in the batter, spoon the vegetables into the centre and return to the oven. Cook for 30–35 minutes until the batter has risen and set. Serve hot.

VEGETABLE BURGER & CHIPS

>Serves 4 >Preparation time: 50 minutes >Cooking time: 55 minutes

INGREDIENTS

BURGERS

100 g/3½ oz spinach

1 tbsp olive oil

1 leek, chopped

2 garlic cloves, crushed

100 g/3½ oz mushrooms, chopped

300 g/10½ oz firm tofu, chopped

1 tsp chilli powder

1 tsp curry powder

1 tbsp chopped fresh coriander

75 g/2¾ oz fresh wholemeal breadcrumbs

1 tbsp olive oil

burger bap or roll with salad, to serve

CHIPS

2 large potatoes

2 tbsp flour

1 tsp chilli powder

2 tbsp olive oil

METHOD

1 To make the burgers, cook the spinach in a little water for 2 minutes. Drain thoroughly and pat dry with kitchen paper.

2 Heat the oil in a frying pan and sauté the leek and garlic for 2–3 minutes. Add the remaining ingredients except the breadcrumbs and cook for 5–7 minutes. Toss in the spinach and cook for 1 minute.

3 Transfer the mixture to a blender and process until almost smooth, mix in the breadcrumbs, and leave until cool enough to handle. With floured hands, form the mixture into four equal-sized burgers. Chill for 30 minutes.

4 To make the chips, cut the potatoes into thin wedges and cook in a pan of boiling water for 10 minutes. Drain and toss in the flour and chilli powder. Lay the chips on a baking tray and sprinkle with the oil. Cook in a preheated oven, 200°C/400°F/Gas Mark 6, for 30 minutes.

5 Meanwhile, heat 1 tablespoon of oil in a frying pan. Cook the burgers for 8–10 minutes, turning once. Serve with salad in a bap, with the chips on the side.

STUFFED MUSHROOMS

›Serves 4   ›Preparation time: 15 minutes   ›Cooking time: 25 minutes

INGREDIENTS

8 open-cap mushrooms

1 tbsp olive oil

1 small leek, chopped

1 celery stick, chopped

100 g/3½ oz firm tofu, diced

1 courgette, chopped

1 carrot, chopped

100 g/3½ oz fresh wholemeal breadcrumbs

2 tbsp chopped basil

1 tbsp tomato purée

2 tbsp pine kernels

75 g/2¾ oz vegetarian Cheddar cheese, grated

150 ml/5 fl oz vegetable stock

salt and pepper

green salad, to serve

METHOD

1 Remove the stalks from the mushrooms. Chop the stalks finely and set aside, then place the whole mushrooms, undersides up, in a shallow ovenproof dish.

2 Heat the oil in a frying pan. Add the chopped mushroom stalks, leek, celery, tofu, courgette and carrot and cook for 3–4 minutes, stirring.

3 Stir in the breadcrumbs, basil, tomato purée and pine kernels. Season with salt and pepper to taste.

4 Spoon the mixture into the mushrooms in the ovenproof dish and top with the cheese. Pour the stock around the mushrooms.

5 Cook in a preheated oven, 220°C/425°F/ Gas Mark 7, for 20 minutes or until cooked through and the cheese has melted. Remove the mushrooms from the dish and serve hot with a green salad.

VEGETABLE BIRYANI

>Serves 4   >Preparation time: 2¼ hours   >Cooking time: 1 hour

INGREDIENTS

1 large potato, cubed

100 g/3½ oz baby carrots

50 g/1¼ oz okra, thickly sliced

2 celery sticks, sliced

75 g/2¼ oz baby button mushrooms, halved

1 aubergine, halved and sliced

300 ml/10 fl oz natural yogurt

1 tbsp grated fresh root ginger

2 large onions, grated

4 garlic cloves, crushed

1 tsp turmeric

1 tbsp curry powder

2 tbsp butter

2 onions, sliced

225 g/8 oz basmati rice

chopped coriander, to garnish

METHOD

1 Cook the potato cubes, carrots and okra in a pan of boiling salted water for 7–8 minutes. Drain well and place in a large bowl. Mix with the celery, mushrooms and aubergine.

2 Mix the natural yogurt, ginger, grated onions, garlic, turmeric and curry powder and spoon over the vegetables. Leave to marinate for at least 2 hours.

3 Heat the butter in a frying pan and cook the sliced onions for 5–6 minutes until golden brown. Remove a few onions from the pan and reserve for garnishing.

4 Cook the rice in a pan of boiling water for 7 minutes. Drain well.

5 Add the marinated vegetables to the onions and cook for 10 minutes.

6 Put half of the rice in a 2-litre/3½-pint casserole dish. Spoon the vegetables on top and cover them with the remaining rice. Cover and cook in a preheated oven, 190°C/375°F/Gas Mark 5, for 20–25 minutes or until the rice is just tender.

7 Spoon the biryani on to a serving plate, garnish with the reserved onions and chopped coriander and serve hot.

CAULIFLOWER BAKE

> Serves 4 > Preparation time: 10 minutes > Cooking time: 35 minutes

INGREDIENTS

450 g/1 lb cauliflower, broken into florets

2 large potatoes, cubed

100 g/3½ oz cherry tomatoes

SAUCE

2 tbsp butter or vegetarian margarine

1 leek, sliced

1 garlic clove, crushed

25 g/1 oz plain flour

300 ml/10 fl oz milk

75 g/2¾ oz mixed grated cheese, such as
vegetarian Cheddar, Parmesan and Gruyère

½ tsp paprika

2 tbsp chopped fresh flat-leaved parsley, plus
extra to garnish

salt and pepper

METHOD

1 Cook the cauliflower in a saucepan of boiling
water for 10 minutes. Drain well and reserve.
Meanwhile, cook the potatoes in a pan of
boiling water for 10 minutes, drain and reserve.

2 To make the sauce, melt the butter or
margarine in a saucepan and sauté the leek
and garlic for 1 minute. Add the flour and cook
for 1 minute. Remove the pan from the heat
and gradually stir in the milk, 50 g/1¼ oz of the
cheese, and the paprika and parsley. Return the
pan to the heat and bring to the boil, stirring.
Season with salt and pepper to taste.

3 Spoon the cauliflower into a deep ovenproof
dish. Add the cherry tomatoes and top with
the potatoes. Pour the sauce over the potatoes
and sprinkle on the remaining cheese.

4 Cook in a preheated oven, 180°C/350°F/Gas
Mark 4, for 20 minutes or until the vegetables
are cooked through and the cheese is golden
brown and bubbling. Garnish with chopped
parsley and serve hot.

VEGETABLE ENCHILADAS

>Serves 4 >Preparation time: 10 minutes >Cooking time: 50 minutes

INGREDIENTS

4 flour tortillas

75 g/2¾ oz vegetarian Cheddar cheese, grated

FILLING

75 g/2¾ oz spinach

2 tbsp olive oil

8 baby sweetcorn cobs, sliced

25 g/1 oz frozen peas, defrosted

1 red pepper, diced

1 carrot, diced

1 leek, sliced

2 garlic cloves, crushed

1 red chilli, chopped

salt and pepper

SAUCE

300 ml/10 fl oz passata

2 shallots, chopped

1 garlic clove, crushed

300 ml/10 fl oz vegetable stock

1 tsp caster sugar

1 tsp chilli powder

METHOD

1 To make the filling, blanch the spinach in a pan of boiling water for 2 minutes, drain well and chop.

2 Heat the oil in a frying pan and sauté the corn, peas, pepper, carrot, leek, garlic and chilli for 3–4 minutes, stirring briskly. Stir in the spinach and season to taste.

3 Put all of the sauce ingredients in a saucepan and bring to the boil, stirring. Cook over a high heat for 20 minutes, stirring, until thickened and reduced by a third.

4 Spoon a quarter of the filling along the centre of each tortilla. Roll the tortillas around the filling and place in an ovenproof dish, seam-side down.

5 Pour the sauce over the tortillas and sprinkle the cheese on top. Cook in a preheated oven, 180°C/350°F/Gas Mark 4, for 20 minutes or until the cheese has melted and browned. Serve hot.

FALAFEL

>Serves 4 >Preparation time: 25 minutes >Cooking time: 10–15 minutes

INGREDIENTS

650 g/1 lb 7 oz canned chick-peas, drained

1 red onion, chopped

3 garlic cloves, crushed

100 g/3½ oz wholemeal bread

2 small red chillies

1 tsp ground cumin

1 tsp ground coriander

½ tsp turmeric

1 tbsp chopped coriander, plus extra to garnish

1 egg, beaten

100 g/3½ oz fresh wholemeal breadcrumbs

vegetable oil, for deep-frying

salt and pepper

TO SERVE

tomato and cucumber salad

lemon wedges

METHOD

1 Put the chick-peas, onion, garlic, bread, chillies, spices and coriander in a food processor and blend for 30 seconds. Stir and season well.

2 Remove the mixture from the food processor and shape into walnut-sized balls.

3 Place the beaten egg in a shallow bowl and place the wholemeal breadcrumbs on a plate. Dip the balls into the egg to coat and then roll in the breadcrumbs, shaking off any excess.

4 Heat the oil for deep-frying to 180°C/350°F, or until a cube of bread browns in 30 seconds. Fry the falafel, in batches, for 2–3 minutes until crisp and browned. Remove from the oil with a slotted spoon and dry on kitchen paper. Garnish with coriander and serve with tomato and cucumber salad and lemon wedges.

NUT ROAST WITH TOMATO SAUCE

>Serves 4   >Preparation time: 15 minutes   >Cooking time: 1 hour 20 minutes

INGREDIENTS

450 g/1 lb floury potatoes, diced

2 tbsp butter

1 onion, chopped

2 garlic cloves, crushed

115 g/4 oz unsalted peanuts

85 g/3 oz fresh white breadcrumbs

1 egg, beaten

2 tbsp chopped fresh coriander

150 ml/5 fl oz vegetable stock

85 g/3 oz mushrooms, sliced

55 g/2 oz sun-dried tomatoes in oil, drained and sliced

salt and pepper

SAUCE

150 ml/5 fl oz crème fraîche

2 tsp tomato purée

2 tsp clear honey

2 tbsp chopped fresh coriander

METHOD

1 Grease a 450-g/1-lb loaf tin. Cook the potatoes in a saucepan of boiling water for 10 minutes until cooked through. Drain well, mash and set aside.

2 Melt half of the butter in a frying pan. Add the onion and garlic and fry for 2–3 minutes until soft. In a food processor, process the nuts for 30 seconds with the breadcrumbs.

3 Mix the nuts and breadcrumbs into the potatoes with the egg, coriander and stock. Stir in the onion and garlic and mix well.

4 Melt the remaining butter in the frying pan, add the mushrooms and cook for 2–3 minutes.

5 Press half of the potato mixture into the base of the loaf tin. Spoon the mushrooms on top and sprinkle with sun-dried tomatoes. Smooth the remaining potato mixture on top. Cover with foil and bake in a preheated oven, 190°C/375°F/Gas Mark 5, for 1 hour or until firm.

6 Meanwhile, mix the sauce ingredients. Slice the nut roast and serve with the sauce.

CHEESE & POTATO LAYER BAKE

>Serves 4 >Preparation time: 20 minutes >Cooking time: 1¼–1½ hours

INGREDIENTS

450 g/1 lb potatoes

1 leek, sliced

3 garlic cloves, crushed

50 g/1¼ oz Cheddar cheese, grated

50 g/1¼ oz mozzarella cheese, grated

25 g/1 oz freshly grated Parmesan cheese

2 tbsp chopped fresh parsley

150 ml/5 fl oz single cream

150 ml/5 fl oz milk

salt and pepper

chopped fresh flat-leaved parsley, to garnish

METHOD

1 Cook the potatoes in a saucepan of boiling salted water for 10 minutes. Drain well.

2 Cut the potatoes into thin slices. Arrange a layer of potatoes in the base of an ovenproof dish. Layer with a little of the leek, garlic, cheeses and parsley. Season well.

3 Repeat the layers until all of the ingredients have been used, finishing with a layer of cheese on top.

4 Mix the cream and milk together, season with salt and pepper to taste and pour over the potato layers.

5 Cook in a preheated oven, 160°C/325°F/Gas Mark 3, for 1–1¼ hours or until the cheese is golden brown and bubbling and the potatoes are cooked through.

6 Garnish with chopped flat-leaved parsley and serve hot.

MACARONI CHEESE & TOMATO

>Serves 4 >Preparation time: 15 minutes >Cooking time: 35–40 minutes

INGREDIENTS

225 g/8 oz dried elbow macaroni

175 g/6 oz Cheddar cheese, grated

100 g/3½ oz freshly grated Parmesan cheese

4 tbsp fresh white breadcrumbs

1 tbsp chopped fresh basil

1 tbsp butter or margarine

TOMATO SAUCE

1 tbsp olive oil

1 shallot, finely chopped

2 garlic cloves, crushed

500 g/1 lb 2 oz canned chopped tomatoes

1 tbsp chopped fresh basil

salt and pepper

METHOD

1 To make the tomato sauce, heat the oil in a heavy-based saucepan. Add the shallot and garlic and sauté for 1 minute. Add the tomatoes and basil and season with salt and pepper to taste. Cook over a medium heat, stirring constantly, for 10 minutes.

2 Meanwhile, bring a large saucepan of lightly salted water to the boil and cook the macaroni for 8 minutes, or until tender, but still firm to the bite. Drain thoroughly and set aside.

3 Mix the Cheddar and Parmesan together in a bowl. Grease a deep, ovenproof dish. Spoon one-third of the tomato sauce into the base of the dish, top with one-third of the macaroni and then one-third of the cheeses. Season to taste with salt and pepper. Repeat these layers twice, ending with a layer of grated cheese.

4 Combine the breadcrumbs and basil and sprinkle evenly over the top. Dot the topping with butter or margarine and cook in a preheated oven, 190°C/375°F/Gas Mark 5, for 25 minutes, or until the the topping is golden brown and bubbling. Serve hot.

21

SPANISH TORTILLA

>Serves 4   >Preparation time: 10 minutes   >Cooking time: 30–35 minutes

INGREDIENTS

1 kg/2 lb 4 oz waxy potatoes, thinly sliced

4 tbsp vegetable oil

1 onion, sliced

2 garlic cloves, crushed

1 green pepper, deseeded and diced

2 tomatoes, deseeded and chopped

25 g/1 oz drained canned sweetcorn

6 large eggs, beaten

2 tbsp chopped fresh parsley

salt and pepper

METHOD

1 Parboil the potatoes in a saucepan of lightly salted boiling water for 5 minutes. Drain well.

2 Heat the oil in a large frying pan, add the potato and onion and sauté over a low heat, stirring constantly, for 5 minutes, or until the potatoes have browned.

3 Add the garlic, diced pepper, chopped tomatoes and sweetcorn, mixing well.

4 Pour in the eggs and add the chopped parsley. Season well with salt and pepper. Cook for 10–12 minutes, or until the underside is cooked through.

5 Remove the frying pan from the heat and continue to cook the tortilla under a preheated medium grill for 5–7 minutes, or until the tortilla is set and the top is golden brown.

6 Cut the tortilla into wedges or cubes, depending on your preference, and transfer to serving dishes. In Spain, tortillas are served hot, cold or warm.

MEDITERRANEAN PEPPERS

>Serves 6   >Preparation time: 15 minutes   >Cooking time: 1 hour 5 minutes

INGREDIENTS

6 large peppers, red, yellow and orange

200 g/7 oz long-grain white rice

2–3 tbsp olive oil, plus extra for drizzling

1 large onion

2 celery sticks, chopped

2 garlic cloves, finely chopped

1/2 tsp ground cinnamon or allspice

75 g/2 3/4 oz raisins

4 tbsp pine kernels, lightly toasted

4 ripe plum tomatoes, deseeded and chopped

50 ml/2 fl oz white wine

4 anchovy fillets, chopped

1/2 bunch of fresh parsley, chopped

1/2 bunch of fresh mint, chopped

100 g/3 1/2 oz freshly grated Parmesan cheese

salt and pepper

tomato sauce, to serve (see page 21)

METHOD

1 Using a sharp knife, slice off the tops of the peppers, then remove the cores and the seeds. Blanch the peppers in boiling water for 2–3 minutes. Carefully remove and drain upside-down on a wire rack.

2 Cook the rice in boiling salted water until tender, but firm to the bite. Drain and rinse under cold running water.

3 Heat the oil in a large frying pan. Add the onion and celery and cook for 2 minutes. Stir in the garlic, cinnamon and raisins and cook for 1 minute. Fork in the rice, then stir in the pine kernels, tomatoes, wine, anchovies, parsley and mint and cook for 4 minutes. Remove from the heat, add salt and pepper to taste and stir in half the Parmesan cheese.

4 Brush the bottom of an ovenproof dish with oil. Divide the rice mixture equally among the peppers. Arrange in the dish and sprinkle with the remaining Parmesan. Drizzle with a little more oil and pour in enough water to come 1 cm/1/2 inch up the sides of the peppers. Loosely cover the dish with kitchen foil.

5 Bake in a preheated oven, 180°C/350°F/Gas Mark, 4 for about 40 minutes. Uncover and cook for a further 10 minutes. Serve hot with tomato sauce.

VEGETABLE CANNELLONI

›Serves 4 ›Preparation time: 10 minutes ›Cooking time: 45 minutes

INGREDIENTS

1 aubergine

125 ml/4 fl oz olive oil

225 g/8 oz spinach

2 garlic cloves, crushed

1 tsp ground cumin

75 g/2¼ oz mushrooms, chopped

12 cannelloni tubes

50 g/1¼ oz mozzarella cheese, sliced

salt and pepper

TOMATO SAUCE

1 tbsp olive oil

1 onion, chopped

2 garlic cloves, crushed

2 x 400 g/14 oz cans chopped tomatoes

1 tsp caster sugar

2 tbsp chopped fresh basil

METHOD

1 Cut the aubergine into small dice. Heat the oil in a frying pan, add the aubergine and cook for 2–3 minutes.

2 Add the spinach, crushed garlic, cumin and mushrooms to the pan. Season and cook for 2–3 minutes, stirring. Spoon the mixture into the cannelloni tubes and place in an ovenproof dish in a single layer.

3 To make the sauce, heat the olive oil in a saucepan and sauté the onion and garlic for 1 minute. Add the tomatoes, caster sugar and chopped basil and bring to the boil. Reduce the heat and simmer for 5 minutes. Pour the sauce over the cannelloni tubes.

4 Arrange the sliced mozzarella cheese on top of the sauce and cook in a preheated oven, 190°C/375°F/Gas Mark 5, for 30 minutes or until the cheese is bubbling and golden brown. Serve hot.

CASHEW NUT PAELLA

>Serves 4 >Preparation time: 5 minutes >Cooking time: 35 minutes

INGREDIENTS

2 tbsp olive oil

1 tbsp butter

1 red onion, chopped

150 g/5½ oz arborio rice

1 tsp ground turmeric

1 tsp ground cumin

½ tsp chilli powder

3 garlic cloves, crushed

1 green chilli, sliced

1 green pepper, deseeded and diced

1 red pepper, deseeded and diced

75 g/2¾ oz baby corn cobs, halved lengthways

2 tbsp stoned black olives

1 large tomato, deseeded and diced

450 ml/16 fl oz vegetable stock

75 g/2¾ oz unsalted cashew nuts

25 g/1 oz frozen peas

2 tbsp chopped fresh parsley

pinch of cayenne pepper

salt and pepper

fresh herbs, to garnish

METHOD

1 Heat the olive oil and butter in a large frying pan or paella pan until the butter has melted.

2 Add the chopped onion to the pan and sauté for 2–3 minutes, stirring, until softened.

3 Stir in the rice, turmeric, cumin, chilli powder, garlic, chilli, peppers, corn cobs, olives and tomato and cook over a medium heat for 1–2 minutes, stirring occasionally.

4 Pour in the stock and bring the mixture to the boil. Reduce the heat and cook for 20 minutes, stirring.

5 Add the cashew nuts and frozen peas to the mixture in the pan and cook for a further 5 minutes, stirring occasionally. Season to taste and sprinkle with parsley and cayenne pepper. Transfer to warm serving plates, garnish with herbs and serve hot.

COURGETTE & MIXED PEPPER FLAN

›Serves 6–8 ›Preparation time: 10–15 minutes ›Cooking time: 50–55 minutes

INGREDIENTS

250 g/9 oz ready-made fresh puff pastry

3 tbsp olive oil

2 red peppers, deseeded and diced

2 green peppers, deseeded and diced

150 ml/5 fl oz double cream

1 egg

2 courgettes, sliced

salt and pepper

METHOD

1 Roll out the pastry on a lightly floured surface and use it to line a 20-cm/8-inch loose-bottomed flan tin. Leave to chill in the refrigerator for 20 minutes.

2 Meanwhile, heat 2 tablespoons of the olive oil in a pan and fry the peppers for 8 minutes, or until softened, stirring frequently.

3 Whisk the double cream and egg together in a bowl and season to taste with salt and pepper. Stir in the cooked peppers.

4 Heat the remaining oil in a pan and fry the courgette slices for 4–5 minutes, or until lightly browned.

5 Pour the egg and pepper mixture into the pastry case.

6 Arrange the courgette slices around the edge of the tart.

7 Bake in a preheated oven, 180°C/350°F/Gas Mark 4, for 35–40 minutes, or until just set and golden brown.

GNOCCHI WITH TOMATOES & HERBS

>Serves 4 >Preparation time: 30 minutes >Cooking time: 45 minutes

INGREDIENTS

350 g/12 oz floury potatoes (suitable for baking or mashing), halved

75 g/2¼ oz self-raising flour, plus extra for dusting

2 tsp dried oregano

2 tbsp oil

1 large onion, chopped

2 garlic cloves, chopped

400 g/14 oz canned chopped tomatoes

½ vegetable stock cube dissolved in 100ml/3½ fl oz boiling water

2 tbsp shredded fresh basil, plus whole leaves to garnish

salt and pepper

freshly grated Parmesan cheese, to serve

METHOD

1 Bring a large pan of water to the boil. Add the potatoes and cook for 12–15 minutes, or until tender. Drain and leave to cool.

2 Peel and then mash the potatoes with the salt and pepper, sifted flour and oregano. Mix together with your hands to form a dough.

3 Heat the oil in a pan. Add the onion and garlic and cook for 3–4 minutes. Add the tomatoes and stock and cook, uncovered, for 10 minutes. Season to taste.

4 Roll the potato dough into a sausage about 2.5 cm/1 inch in diameter. Cut the sausage into 2.5 cm/1 inch lengths. Flour your hands, then press a fork into each piece to create a series of ridges on one side and the indent of your index finger on the other.

5 Bring a large pan of water to the boil and cook the gnocchi, in batches, for 2–3 minutes. They should rise to the surface when cooked. Drain and keep warm.

6 Stir the basil into the tomato sauce and pour over the gnocchi. Garnish with basil leaves and freshly ground black pepper. Sprinkle with Parmesan and serve.

27

VEGETABLE HOT POT

>Serves 4   >Preparation time: 10 minutes   >Cooking time: 50–55 minutes

INGREDIENTS

2 large potatoes, thinly sliced

2 tbsp vegetable oil

1 red onion, halved and sliced

1 leek, sliced

2 garlic cloves, crushed

1 carrot, cut into chunks

100 g/3½ oz broccoli florets

100 g/3½ oz cauliflower florets

2 small turnips, quartered

1 tbsp plain flour

700 ml/1¼ pints vegetable stock

150 ml/5 fl oz dry cider

1 dessert apple, sliced

2 tbsp chopped fresh sage

pinch of cayenne pepper

50 g/1¾ oz vegetarian Cheddar cheese, grated

salt and pepper

METHOD

1 Cook the potato slices in a saucepan of boiling water for 10 minutes. Drain thoroughly and reserve.

2 Heat the oil in a flameproof casserole dish and sauté the onion, leek and garlic for 2–3 minutes. Add the remaining vegetables and cook for a further 3–4 minutes, stirring.

3 Stir in the flour and cook for 1 minute. Gradually add the stock and cider and bring the mixture to the boil. Add the apple, sage and cayenne pepper and season well. Remove the dish from the heat. Transfer the vegetables to an ovenproof dish.

4 Arrange the potato slices on top of the vegetable mixture to cover.

5 Sprinkle the cheese on top of the potato slices and cook in a preheated oven, 190°C/375°F/Gas Mark 5, for 30–35 minutes or until the potato is golden brown and beginning to crispen slightly around the edges. Serve hot.

WILD MUSHROOM RISOTTO

> Serves 6 > Preparation time: 35 minutes > Cooking time: 35 minutes

INGREDIENTS

55 g/2 oz dried porcini or morel mushrooms

about 500 g/1 lb 2 oz mixed fresh wild mushrooms, such as porcini, girolles, horse mushrooms and chanterelles, halved if large

4 tbsp olive oil

3–4 garlic cloves, finely chopped

4 tbsp unsalted butter

1 onion, finely chopped

350 g/12 oz arborio or carnaroli rice

50 ml/2 fl oz dry white vermouth

1.2 litres/2 pints vegetable stock, simmering

115 g/4 oz freshly grated Parmesan cheese

4 tbsp chopped fresh flat-leaved parsley

salt and pepper

METHOD

1 Place the dried mushrooms in a bowl and add boiling water to cover. Set aside to soak for 30 minutes, then carefully lift out and pat dry. Strain the soaking liquid through a sieve lined with kitchen paper and set aside.

2 Trim the wild mushrooms. Brush them clean.

3 Heat 3 tablespoons of the oil in a large frying pan. Add the wild mushrooms and stir-fry for 1–2 minutes. Add the garlic and the soaked mushrooms and cook, stirring frequently, for 2 minutes. Transfer to a plate.

4 Heat the remaining oil and 2 tablespoons of the butter in a large heavy-based saucepan. Add the onion and cook, stirring occasionally, for about 2 minutes until softened. Add the rice and cook, stirring frequently, for about 2 minutes until translucent and well coated.

5 Add the vermouth. When almost absorbed, add a ladleful (about 225 ml/8 fl oz) of the stock. Cook, stirring constantly, until the liquid is absorbed.

6 Continue adding the stock, about half a ladleful at a time, allowing each addition to be completely absorbed before adding the next. This should take 20–25 minutes. The risotto should have a creamy consistency and the rice should be tender, but firm to the bite.

7 Add half the reserved mushroom soaking liquid to the risotto and stir in the mushrooms. Season with salt and pepper to taste and add more mushroom liquid if necessary. Remove the pan from the heat and stir in the remaining butter, the grated Parmesan and chopped parsley. Serve hot.

VEGETABLE LASAGNE

> Serves 4 > Preparation time: 50 minutes > Cooking time: 45–55 minutes

INGREDIENTS

1 kg/2 lb 4 oz aubergines

125 ml/4 fl oz olive oil

2 tbsp garlic and herb butter

450 g/1 lb courgettes, sliced

225 g/8 oz mozzarella cheese, grated

600 ml/1 pint passata

6 sheets pre-cooked green lasagne

600 ml/1 pint home-made or packet-mix béchamel sauce

55 g/2 oz freshly grated Parmesan cheese

1 tsp dried oregano

salt and black pepper

METHOD

1 Thinly slice the aubergines and place in a colander. Sprinkle with salt and set aside for 20 minutes. Rinse, then dry with kitchen paper.

2 Heat half of the oil in a large frying pan. Fry half the aubergine slices over a low heat for 6–7 minutes, or until golden. Drain on kitchen paper. Repeat with the remaining oil and aubergine slices. Set aside.

3 Melt the garlic and herb butter in the frying pan, add the sliced courgettes and fry for 5–6 minutes, or until golden brown all over. Drain on kitchen paper.

4 Place half the aubergine and courgette slices in a large ovenproof dish. Season with pepper and sprinkle over half the mozzarella cheese. Spoon over half the passata and top with 3 sheets of lasagne. Repeat the process, ending with a layer of lasagne.

5 Spoon over the béchamel sauce and sprinkle over the Parmesan cheese and oregano. Put the dish on a baking tray and bake in a preheated oven, 220°C/425°F/Gas Mark 7, for 30–35 minutes, or until golden brown. Serve hot.